Mining

Tatiana Tomljanovic

Weigl

CALGARY
www.weigl.com

Published by Weigl Educational Publishers Limited
6325 10 Street S.E.
Calgary, Alberta T2H 2Z9

Library of Congress Cataloging-in-Publication Data

Tomljanovic, Tatiana
    Mining / Tatiana Tomljanovic.
(Linking Canadian communities)
Includes index.
ISBN 978-1-55388-383-8 (bound)
ISBN 978-1-55388-384-5 (pbk.)
    1. Mineral industries--Canada--Juvenile literature. 2. Mineral
industries--Economic aspects--Canada--Juvenile literature. 3. Mineral
industries--Canada--History--Juvenile literature. I. Title. II. Series.
HD9506.C22T64 2007   j338.20971   C2007-902254-5

Printed in the United States of America
1 2 3 4 5 6 7 8 9 11 10 09 08 07

Editor
Heather C. Hudak
Design
Warren Clark

All of the Internet URLs given in the book were valid at the time of publication. However, due to the
dynamic nature of the Internet, some addresses may have changed, or sites may have ceased to exist
since publication. While the author and publisher regret any inconvenience this may cause readers,
no responsibility for any such changes can be accepted by either the author or the publisher.

Every reasonable effort has been made to trace ownership and to obtain permission to reprint copyright
material. The publishers would be pleased to have any errors or omissions brought to their attention so
that they may be corrected in subsequent printings.

We acknowledge the financial support of the Government of Canada through the Book Publishing
Industry Development Program (BPIDP) for our publishing activities.

Contents

What is a Community? 4

Welcome to a Mining Community 6

The Mining Industry 8

Diamond Processing 10

Canada's Mining Map 12

Careers 14

Links Between Communities 16

The Environment 18

Brain Teasers 20

Chocolate Chip Mine 22

Further Research 23

Words To Know/Index 24

What is a Community?

A community is a place where people live, work, and play together. There are large and small communities.

Small communities are also called rural communities. These communities have fewer people and less traffic than large communities. There is plenty of open space.

Large communities are called towns or cities. These are urban communities. They have taller buildings and more cars, stores, and people than rural communities.

Canada has many types of communities. Some have forests for logging. Others have farms. There are also fishing, energy, **manufacturing**, and mining communities.

▶ Types of Canadian Communities

FARMING COMMUNITIES
- use the land to grow crops, such as wheat, barley, canola, fruits, and vegetables
- some raise livestock, such as cattle, sheep, and pigs

ENERGY COMMUNITIES
- found near energy sources, such as water, natural gas, oil, coal, and uranium
- have **natural resources**
- provide power for homes and businesses

FISHING COMMUNITIES
- found along Canada's 202,080 kilometres of coastline
- fishers catch fish, lobster, shrimp, and other sea life

Real Canadian Communities

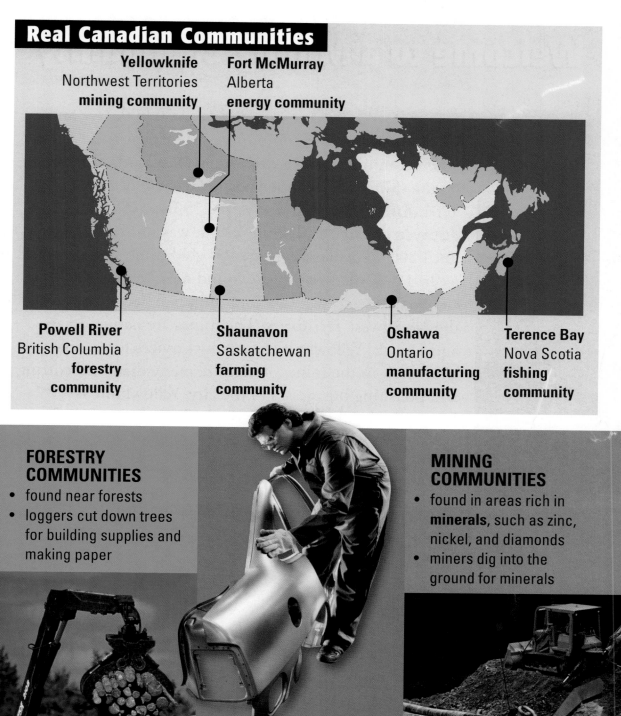

Yellowknife
Northwest Territories
mining community

Fort McMurray
Alberta
energy community

Powell River
British Columbia
forestry community

Shaunavon
Saskatchewan
farming community

Oshawa
Ontario
manufacturing community

Terence Bay
Nova Scotia
fishing community

FORESTRY COMMUNITIES
- found near forests
- loggers cut down trees for building supplies and making paper

MINING COMMUNITIES
- found in areas rich in **minerals**, such as zinc, nickel, and diamonds
- miners dig into the ground for minerals

MANUFACTURING COMMUNITIES
- use natural resources to make a finished product
- finished products include cars and computers

Welcome to a Mining Community

Yellowknife has a population of 20,000. It is an urban mining community. Most other mining communities are rural. Yellowknife is located on the shores of Great Slave Lake in the Northwest Territories. It was founded in the 1930s. Gold was discovered near Yellowknife Bay. It was mined there until 2004. At that time, the last gold mine shut down.

In 1991, diamonds were found near Yellowknife. Canada now has two diamond mines. They are both in the Northwest Territories. The mines are named Ekati and Diavik. Yellowknife has many services for people who work in the mines. There are many diamond cutting and polishing businesses in the city. Yellowknife is known as the "Diamond Capital of North America."

Gold mine sites can still be seen in Yellowknife.

First-hand Account

Northwest Territories
Yellowknife ●

Pacific Ocean

| 0 | 200 | 400 kilometres |
| 0 | 200 | 400 miles |

My name is Michael. I have lived in Yellowknife my whole life. I like living here. I take swimming lessons. I like to cross-country ski. I go fishing with my dad on his days off. He works for the Royal Canadian Mounted Police.

It is very cold here in winter. I'm used to it. I know how to dress for the cold. When I walk to school in winter, it is dark. That's because there are only four hours of daylight in the middle of winter. I often see northern lights in the sky at that time of year. In summer, the Sun stays up even when it's late at night. I play outside us much as possible. I like the warm days.

Think About It
Compare Yellowknife to your community.
• How is it the same?
• How is it different?

The Mining Industry

Mining companies dig up minerals and metals. Minerals and metals are **raw materials**. Factories and other businesses turn them into finished products. These include soup cans and jewellery. Salespeople then sell the finished products. Together, all of these businesses are part of the mining industry.

Mining is one of Canada's main industries. The country is the third largest producer of minerals in the world. Canada is the top producer of potash and uranium. There are more than 200 mines, 50 **smelters**, and 3,000 stone, sand, and gravel **pits** in Canada. There are also many **refineries** and steel mills.

Mining communities are found mainly in remote or rural areas.

Timeline

40,000 BC
Copper is traded among Aboriginal Peoples in the Lake Superior area.

998 AD
Vikings mine iron at L'Anse aux Meadows, Newfoundland.

1639
A coal mine opens at Grand Lake, New Brunswick. It is thought to be the first coal mine in North America.

Minerals and metals are important to Canada and the rest of the world. Many items are made out of minerals and metals. There are minerals in toothpaste. They are fluorite, barite, and calcite. Television sets need 35 minerals and metals to make them work. Some of these metals are aluminum, copper, iron, and nickel. There are minerals and metals in almost all manufactured products.

More than 100 Canadian communities across Canada are rooted in the mining industry. Most of these communities are in rural areas.

Mining is an important industry in northern Canada. It gives jobs to people in many communities.

1907
The Canada Department of Mines is formed.

1991
Diamonds are found in the Northwest Territories. It is the first major diamond find in Canada.

2003
About 400,000 Canadians work in the mining industry.

Diamond Processing

Canada's first diamond mine opened in 1998. It is called Ekati. Ekati is 300 kilometres from Yellowknife. Diavik opened in 2001. The Diavik mine is an open-pit mine. This means the diamonds are not underground. At one time, the diamonds were under a lake. Before mining could begin, about 10 billion litres of water were pumped out of the lake. The mine won an award for building a **dike** to hold back the water.

In 2004, Canada was the third largest producer of diamonds in the world. More diamond mines are planned for the Northwest Territories.

The Canadian diamond mining industry is worth $2 billion.

Diamond Process

Geologists discover diamonds.

A diamond mine opens in the area.

Miners dig up rough diamonds. They dig them up from open pits or from underground. Sometimes, they dig more than 1 kilometre below ground.

Diamonds are sorted, based on size, shape, quality, and colour.

Industrial diamonds are used in drills and other tools.

Gem or near-gem quality diamonds are cut and polished, set into jewellery settings, and sold to stores.

Canada's Mining Map

Canada is a big country. It covers nearly 10 million square kilometres. More than 60 types of minerals are mined in Canada. This map shows where the main minerals are found in the country.

Legend

- Potash
- Gold
- Uranium
- Diamonds
- Silver
- Gypsum
- Nickel
- Salt
- Iron
- Sulphur

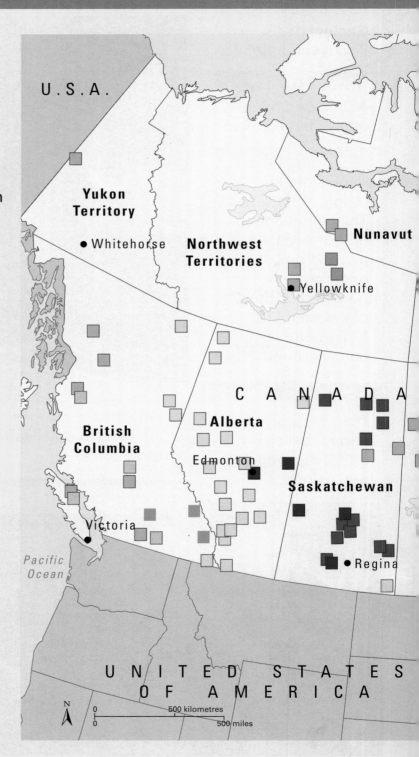

Iqaluit ●

Labrador Sea

Hudson Bay

Manitoba

Newfoundland and Labrador

St. John's ●

Quebec

Ontario

Prince Edward Island

● Winnipeg

New Brunswick

● Charlottetown

Fredericton ●

Nova Scotia

● Quebec City

Halifax ●

Ottawa ★

Atlantic Ocean

● Toronto

Careers

About 400,000 people work in the mining industry in Canada. There are more mining companies in Canada than any other place in the world. Most mining communities are in rural and northern places.

The mining industry creates jobs in other industries. Businesses must **process** raw metals and minerals into finished products. This is called manufacturing. The Canadian mining industry creates more than 250,000 jobs in the manufacturing industry.

———

Computers are often used to show the location of minerals.

There are many types of jobs in the mining industry and its support industries. For example, geologists search for rocks with certain minerals and metals. They help decide where mines should be built. Miners drill for the minerals and metals.

Jewellers turn diamonds into jewellery. They cut the diamonds. Then, they make them into necklaces, earrings, and other pieces of jewellery.

Surveyors measure the layout of the mine.

Think About It
What other jobs might there be in the mining industry?

Links Between Communities

Everyone is part of a community. It may be a village, a town, or a city. Communities are linked to one another. Each Canadian community uses goods that link it to other communities. Goods are things people grow, make, or gather to use or sell.

A forestry community makes lumber for construction. The wood may be shipped to another community to build houses or furniture.

Energy communities produce natural gas, oil, and other types of energy, such as wind, solar, and hydro. Other communities use this energy to power their homes and vehicles.

Dairy products and meats come from farming communities that raise cattle and other animals. People in all communities drink milk products and eat meat from these communities. Many farming communities grow crops such as wheat. Wheat is used to make bread and pastries.

These goods may be fish, grains, cars, and paper products. Communities depend on one another for goods and services. A service is useful work that is done to meet the needs of others. People are linked when they use the goods and services provided by others.

Manufacturing communities make products such as cars and trucks. They also make airplanes, ships, and trains that are used to transport, or move, people and goods from one place to another. Transportation services help communities build links.

Fishing communities send fish to stores to be bought by people in other places. In Canada, most fish is caught off the Pacific or Atlantic coast. People living on farms or in cities across the country buy the fish at stores.

Diamonds, gold, and potash can be mined. These items are sent from mining communities to other parts of the country. A diamond might be set in a ring for a person in another community.

Think About It

In your community, what goods and services help meet your family's needs and wants?

The Environment

When land is mined, nature can be harmed. Mining can affect land, air, and water systems. Plants are uprooted. Animals lose their homes.

Minerals and metals are non-renewable. Once these minerals have been dug out of the ground, they are gone. There will be nothing left to mine.

Mines can be emptied of all their minerals or metals. These mines are **abandoned**. There are more than 10,000 abandoned mines in Canada. The people who lived near these mines no longer had jobs. They moved away to find work.

Recycling pop cans is one way people can reuse minerals and metals.

Think About It

If mining can damage or destroy land, what will it do to the ocean floor and planets, such as Mars? Should Earth's oceans and Mars be mined?

Scientists and researchers are looking for new places to mine. The ocean and outer space are two such places where this may be possible. Both have minerals and metals. Ocean explorers have found jets of very hot water. They rise from cracks in the ocean floor. These jets sometimes carry minerals from deep within Earth. Rock samples were collected on **expeditions** to the Moon and Mars. Scientists studied the samples. The Moon and Mars may be sources of minerals for future mining.

Eco-friendly Recycling

Canada is beginning to run out of metals to mine. Until new metal deposits are found, Canada can reduce the metal shortage by **recycling**. Any scrap of leftover metal can be recycled. Pop cans and other drink containers are collected for recycling. Most Canadian cities and towns have bottle depots. People can bring their empty bottles or cans to their local bottle depot for recycling. Bottle depots pay for each recyclable drink container.

Brain Teasers

Test your knowledge by trying to answer these brain teasers.

Q *Scientists and researchers are looking for new areas to mine. Where are they looking?*

A They are looking into the possibility of mining the ocean floor and outer space.

Q *Name three types of communities in Canada.*

A Canada has forestry communities, farming communities, fishing communities, energy communities, mining communities, and manufacturing communities.

Q *What two things link communities?*

A Goods and services link communities.

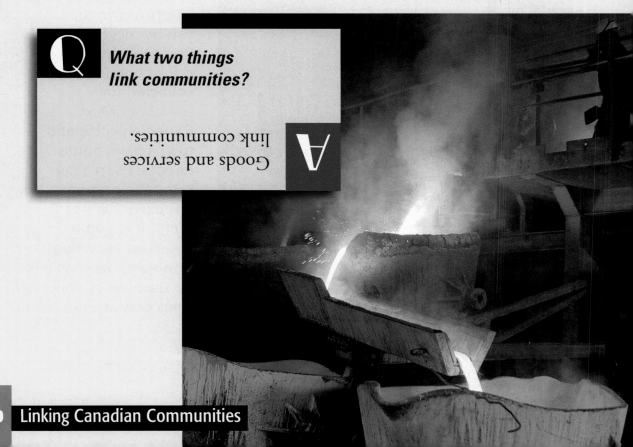

Q *Name the two diamond mines in the Northwest Territories.*

A Ekati and Diavik are the two diamond mines in the Northwest Territories.

Q *What is the difference between a rural and an urban community?*

A A rural community has plenty of open space and few people. An urban community has many buildings and more people.

Q *Where is Yellowknife located?*

A Yellowknife is in the Northwest Territories.

Chocolate Chip Mine

How well can you dig for valuable minerals without damaging the environment? Test your skills with the following mining activity. Instead of digging for gold or diamonds, you will dig for chocolate chips.

Materials

- 2 chocolate chip cookies
- 2 toothpicks
- stopwatch or timer

Procedure

1. Take one cookie, and pretend it is an environment in which a valuable mineral has been found (chocolate chips).
2. Using the toothpicks, remove as many chocolate chips as possible in 2 minutes. Time yourself using a stopwatch or timer.
3. Count the number of chocolate chips you mined. How many are there?
4. Now look at the impact of your mining activity on the cookie "environment." What do you think would happen if this were a real mine? What would happen to the animals and plants that lived above the mine you just dug?
5. Mine the second cookie in two minutes, but try not to damage the environment as badly.
6. Make a new pile of chocolate chips.
7. Compare the two piles of chocolate chips. How did you do the second time? You probably "mined" fewer chocolate chips the second time because you tried to do less harm to the environment. Mining companies have to try to get as much from the ground as they can, while limiting the damage they do to Earth.

Further Research

Many books and websites provide information on energy communities. To learn more about energy communities, borrow books from the library, or surf the Internet.

Books

Most libraries have computers that connect to a database for researching information. If you input a key word, you will be provided with a list of books in the library that contain information on that topic. Non-fiction books are arranged numerically, using their call number. Fiction books are organized alphabetically by the author's last name.

Websites

The World Wide Web is also a good source of information. Reliable websites usually include government sites, educational sites, and online encyclopedias.

Learn more about the community of Yellowknife by visiting the city's official website.
www.yellowknife.ca

To watch a cartoon on how diamonds are formed, visit Natural Resources Canada.
www.nrcan.gc.ca/ms/diam/diamform_e.htm

Many of the things that you see around your home are made from minerals and metals. Take a virtual tour of a home to find out what minerals and metals are in plates, mirrors, and computers.
www.nrcan.gc.ca/mms/scho-ecol/tour/intro_e.htm

Words to Know

abandoned: left empty

dike: a high wall of earth built to hold back the waters of a sea, river, or lake

expeditions: journeys made for particular reasons

geologists: people who study the Earth and rocks

manufacturing: making a large amount of an item using machines

minerals: inorganic or unnatural substances found by mining

natural resources: materials found in nature, such as water, soil, and forests, that can be used by people

pits: large holes where stones or minerals are found

process: the series of steps or actions needed to make a new product

raw materials: products that have not yet been made into something else

recycling: finding new ways to reuse materials that have already been used

refineries: factories where substances are processed and purified

smelters: places where ore is melted in order to get metal from it

Index

diamonds 5, 6, 9, 10, 11, 12, 15, 17, 21, 22, 23
Diavik 6, 10, 21

Ekati 6, 10, 21

gold 6, 12, 17, 22

Mars 18, 19
metals 8, 9, 14, 15, 18, 19, 23
minerals 5, 8, 9, 12, 14, 15, 18, 19, 22, 23

Northwest Territories 5, 6, 7, 9, 10, 21

oceans 7, 18, 19, 20

recycling 19
rural 4, 8, 9, 14, 21

urban 4, 6, 21

Yellowknife 5, 6, 7, 9, 10, 21, 23